I spy with my little eye something beginning with .....

It's an

Apple

I spy with my little eye something beginning with .....

It's a

Bouquet

I spy with my little eye something beginning with .....

It's a

Corn

I spy with my little eye something beginning with .....

It's a

Dish

I spy with my little eye something beginning with .....

It's an

Egg

I spy with my little eye something beginning with .....

It's a

Flower

I spy with my little eye something beginning with .....

It's a

Goose

I spy with my little eye something beginning with .....

H

It's

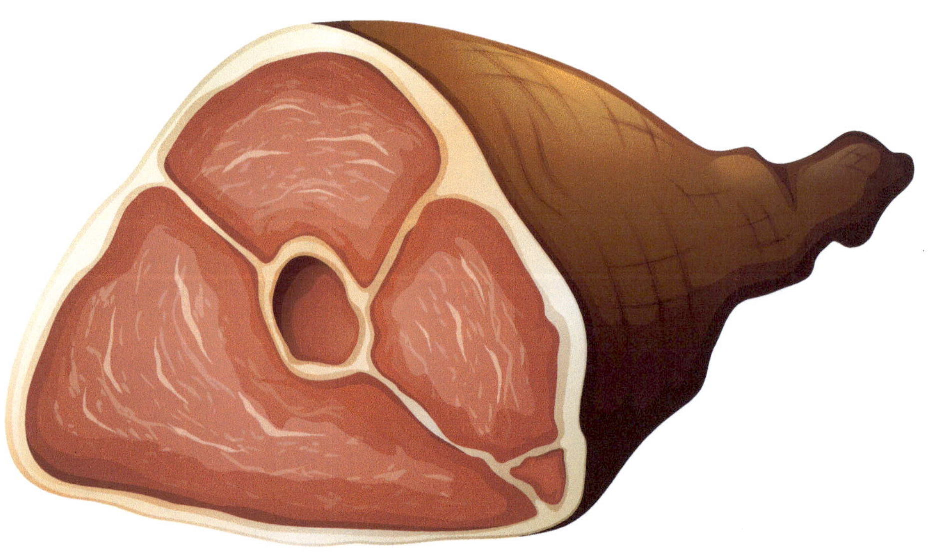

Ham

I spy with my little eye something beginning with .....

It's an

Ice Cream

I spy with my little eye something beginning with .....

It's a

Jam

I spy with my little eye
something beginning with .....

It's a

Kid

I spy with my little eye something beginning with .....

It's a

Leaf

I spy with my little eye something beginning with .....

It's

Maize

I spy with my little eye something beginning with .....

It's

Nuts

I spy with my little eye something beginning with .....

It's an

Oven

I spy with my little eye something beginning with .....

It's a

Pumpkin

I spy with my little eye something beginning with .....

It's a

Quince

I spy with my little eye
something beginning with .....

R

It's a

Raven

I spy with my little eye something beginning with .....

It's a

Squirrel

I spy with my little eye something beginning with .....

It's a

Turkey

I spy with my little eye something beginning with .....

It's a

Unicorn

I spy with my little eye something beginning with ......

It's a

Vanilla

I spy with my little eye something beginning with .....

It's a

Winter

I spy with my little eye something beginning with .....

It's an

Xray Fish

I spy with my little eye something beginning with .....

It's a

Yoghurt

I spy with my little eye something beginning with .....

It's a

Zucchini